T. V. (Thomas Verner) Moore

The Culdee Church

or, The Historical Connection of Modern Presbyterian Churches with..

T. V. (Thomas Verner) Moore

The Culdee Church
or, The Historical Connection of Modern Presbyterian Churches with..

ISBN/EAN: 9783744756556

Printed in Europe, USA, Canada, Australia, Japan

Cover: Foto ©Lupo / pixelio.de

More available books at **www.hansebooks.com**

THE RUINS OF IONA.

THE

CULDEE CHURCH:

OR,

THE HISTORICAL CONNECTION OF MODERN PRESBYTERIAN CHURCHES WITH THOSE OF APOSTOLIC TIMES, THROUGH THE CHURCH OF SCOTLAND.

"ARDENS, SED VIRENS."
"NEC TAMEN CONSUMEBATUR."

BY

REV. T. V. MOORE, D. D.

RICHMOND:

PRESBYTERIAN COMMITTEE OF PUBLICATION.

Introductory Note.

It is proper to say, that the following pages were originally published in the *Central Presbyterian*; and a desire being expressed for their issue in a more permanent form, they are republished almost exactly as they appeared in the newspaper. This will account for some features of the work, which would have been altered, had the author been able to command the time needful for re-writing the articles. These features being of minor importance, are allowed to stand.

CONTENTS.

CHAPTER I.

IONA.

CHAPTER II.

APOSTOLICAL SUCCESSION.

CHAPTER III.

THE PLANTING OF CHRISTIANITY IN SCOTLAND.

CHAPTER IV.

CULDEE PRESBYTERIANISM.

CHAPTER V.

REIGN OF POPERY IN SCOTLAND.

CHAPTER VI.

THE REFORMATION IN SCOTLAND.

CHAPTER VII.

CONCLUDING REFLECTIONS.

THE

CULDEE CHURCH.

CHAPTER I.

IONA.

Its Literary and Historical Interest.

ON the western coast of Scotland, near the bold
juttings of the Ross of Mull, lies a little island, only
two and one-half miles long, by one and one-half
broad, with but a few hundred acres of arable land,
and nothing in its scenery or position to arrest the attention of the traveller. And yet of that bleak islet,
Dr. Johnson, who never spake any thing good of
Scotland that he could avoid, was constrained to
write, " That man is little to be envied, whose patriotism would not gain force on the plains of
Marathon, or whose piety would not grow warmer
among the ruins of *Iona!*" *

There must have been something very marvellous
in the history of a *Scottish* island, which would

* Boswell's Johnson, c. 43, p. 381.

compel the burly dictator of English literature to place it, in relation to religion, beside Marathon in relation to patriotism. We may be very sure that only the undeniable truth of history could have extorted such a tribute from such a man.

What then has woven such a spell of interest around this storm-swept island in the Atlantic? Johnson himself gives it in the same passage when he says, "We were now treading that illustrious island, which was once the luminary of the Caledonian regions, whence savage clans and roving barbarians derived the benefits of knowledge and the blessings of religion." Wordsworth also gives it, in his sonnets on this island, which he calls the "Glory of the West."

"Iona's Saints, forgetting not past days,
    Garlands shall wear of amaranthine bloom,
While heaven's vast sea of voices chants their praise."
"Homeward we turn. Isle of Columba's Cell
    Where Christian piety's soul cheering spark
    (Kindled from Heaven between the light and dark,
Of time) shone like the morning-star, farewell!"*

Campbell, in his beautiful poem of ReuÏlura, gives it also as he writes:

"Star of the morn and eve,
    Reullura shone like thee,
And weil for her might Aodh grieve,
    The dark-attired Culdee.

* Sonnets, Tour in Scotland, xxx—xxxiii.

THE SACRIFICE OF THE DRUIDS.

J CAUGHEY, Sc.

Peace to their shades ! the pure Culdees,
  Where Albyn's earliest priests of God,
Ere yet an island of her seas,
  By foot of Saxon monk was trod,
Long ere her churchmen by bigotry
  Were barred from wedlock's holy tie.
'Twas then that Aodh, famed afar,
  In Iona preached the word with power,
And Reullura, beauty's star,
  Was the partner of his bower."*

Scott, in his Lord of the Isles; Shakspeare, in
Macbeth; and other great writers, have also referred
in striking terms to this Mecca of Scotland.

The main interest that attaches to this island, of
course, centres on the sainted Columba, and the
school of the prophets which he planted there, from
which there went forth such wonderous influences
for good during the darkest ages of the Church's
history. But it has other associations, even older
than that, which invest it with deep interest. It
seems to have been one of the sacred seats of the
ancient religion of the Druids, who had, we have
reason to believe, a Druidic college here, as they
had at Anglesey, in Wales. This form of heathenism was one of peculiar interest; for it was the oldest and purest form in which the primitive Paganism existed ; taking its origin far back on the plains
of Shinar, and carried by the Celtic tribes in their

* Poems, p. 253.

westward migration through the forests of Germany
to the islands of Britain, where its gigantic crom-
lechs, mystic circles and consecrated cairns still
remain to testify the rude and terrible strength of a
religion, which, in spite of its dark cruelties, was
the purest form of the old Pagan religion found on
earth, when Christ came in the flesh. Stonehenge
and Iona are thus strangely linked with the Tower
of Babel and the scattered tribes that were sent
forth from that place, whose clanship and Druidism
are the perverted remains of the patriarchal systems
of government and religion that had their origin in
the family of Noah. As one of the sacred seats of
Druidic learning and religion, Iona has a deep
interest.

But to us the main interest which invests this hallowed isle, is its connection with the Christian history of Scotland, as the seat of the old Culdee
Church, and the College of Columba. This fact
made it a favourite burying place for noble and
royal families, not only of Scotland, but of the
Western isles and of Ireland, unnumbered members
of which were brought to sleep in what was regarded
as the sacred soil of Iona. Kenneth, the first King
of Scotland, properly so called, was buried here,
and many others followed him, ending with Macbeth,
whose tragic story has been immortalized by Shakspeare. This custom of royal interment in Iona,

2

(whose Celtic name was Ii-Cholume-Chille, or Icolmkill,) is put in Macduff's mouth, when he says of the body of the murdered Duncan, that it was

———"Carried to Colmes Kill,
The sacred storehouse of his predecessors,
And guardian of their bones."

It was also the burial-place of the Lords of the Isles, embalmed in the verse of Scott. As the Westminster Abbey of Scotland, it has an interest scarcely less profound than its stately rival on the banks of the Thames, for it claims a hoarier antiquity and a higher sacredness than belongs even to that magnificent treasure-house of England's greatest dead. It was the spiritual and intellectual Pharos of Britain, and much of Northwestern Europe during some of the gloomiest centuries of the dark ages.

But its interest to Presbyterians arises from the relation of the Culdee Church, of which it was the chief seat, to the Apostolic Church on the one hand, and to the Reformation Church on the other, as a historical link connecting the two, and thus giving us a continuous transmission of faithful witnesses, from the earliest times, to the present day. It is with a view of presenting the historical facts bearing on this connection, that we have called attention to this lonely isle of the Atlantic, the Light-house of the North, for some of the darkest centuries in the history of the past.

CHAPTER II.

APOSTOLICAL SUCCESSION.

No Successors to the Apostles—Macaulay's Refutation of the High Church Theory—The only possible and true Apostolical Succession.

BEFORE stating the facts that bear on our connection with the Primitive Church, through the Culdee Church, it may be proper to premise the exact value which we place on such connection, and the only sense in which it can exist as a historical fact.

The phrase "apostolical succession" is one that has been so much used in religious controversy, that it is well to define its precise meaning. There are some who contend for a transmission of the apostolic office to prelates of all later ages, and who affirm that such prelates now are the successors of the Apostles in their apostolate. It is a question we have never seen answered, why these men who say they hold the apostolic office never call themselves Apostles? If they have the office, *a fortiori*, they have the name. Why then do they not take it? When Paul claimed the office, he claimed the name also. Why do they not do the same? Have they any right to reject the name that Christ Himself attached to the office? May we not venture to suggest, that this shrinking from the assumption of the name may be connected with a secret misgiving that after all they have no more right to the office than the name; and that there is a deep significance in the fact that John saw on the foundation of the New Jerusalem the names of only twelve Apostles of the Lamb? The truth is that so plainly does it appear that the office of apostle was an extraordinary and temporary one, demanding that the occupant of it should have seen Jesus after His resurrection, that he might be a witness of this fundamental fact; should have the power of working miracles; and should exercise a jurisdiction over the whole Church, and not a diocese or province; that the instinct of the Christian consciousness has always recoiled from an uninspired man assuming the name apostle, a very significant indication that the thing expressed by that name was never transmitted beyond the first possessors of the office, and hence, that, in that sense, apostolical succession is an impossibility.

But others, who may not claim this, do claim that the only lawful ministry is that which has come down in an unbroken succession of regularly ordained men from the time of the Apostles, and that all other ministerial orders are invalid. This is the Romish and Anglican High-Church position. Perhaps the best disposition of it will be to quote a few paragraphs from the crushing demolition of it, made by one of the most distinguished members of the Church of England, who will not be charged with sectarian bias. Macaulay, in his celebrated review of Gladstone's Church and State, republished in his Miscellanies, has crushed this figment with the hand of a giant. We can only quote a part of his masterly refutation. After demanding the evidence for the alleged fact of apostolical succession in the Church of England, he says: "The transmission of orders from the Apostles to an English clergyman of the present day, must have been through a very great number of intermediate persons. Now it is probable that no clergyman in the Church of England, can trace up his spiritual genealogy, from bishop to bishop, even so far back as the time of the Reformation. There remain fifteen or sixteen hundred years, during which the history of the transmission of orders is buried in utter darkness. And whether he be priest by succession from the Apostles, depends on the question whether, during that long period, some thousands of events took place, any one of which may, without any gross improbability, be supposed not to have taken place. We have not a tittle of evidence to any one of these events. We do not even know the names or countries of the men to whom it is taken for granted that these events happened. We do not know whether the spiritual ancestors of any one of our contemporaries were Spanish or Armenian, Arian or Orthodox. In the utter absence of all particular evidence, we are surely entitled to require that the strictest regularity was observed in every generation, and that episcopal functions. were exercised by none who were not bishops by succession from the Apostles. But we have no such evidence. In the first place we have not full and accurate information touching the polity of the Church during the century which followed the persecution of Nero. The question whether the primitive ecclesiastical constitution bore a greater resemblance to the Anglican or the Calvinistic model, has been fiercely disputed. It is a question on which at least a full half of the ability and erudition of Protestant Europe, has ever since the Reformation, been opposed to the Anglican pretensions. Our author, himself, we are persuaded, would have the candour to allow that if no evidence were admitted but that which is furnished by the genuine Christain literature of the first two centuries, *judgment would not go in favour of prelacy.*" He then, in his own brilliant and unanswerable manner, adduces the proof that the establishment of this claim of the Church of England to apostolical succession in this sense, is simply absurd and impossible. Indeed, it is so untenable, that many of the first men in that

Church, as well as the American Episcopal Church, have rejected it, as may be seen in Dr. Smyth's able work on Apostolical Succession.

The only apostolical succession that is worth any thing is the succession of apostolical truth, of the Gospel, as apostolical men proclaimed it. That is necessary, and fortunately, that does not depend on the hands through which it has been transmitted to us. The truth of the Epistle to the Romans does not depend on whether we received it through thousand hands from Rome, or five thousand hands from Corinth, so that we have the genuine Epistle, any more than the nutritive properties of a loaf of bread depend on our ability to trace it through a baker, miller, merchant, farmer, &c., to the harvest field. If it is bread, it is not the less nutritive because we do not know the pedigree of its transmission. If the Bible is conceded to be the inspired truth of God, it is not less true because we cannot trace the hands through which it passed from the pen that first traced its pages. Now as all parties here in question, concede that we have the genuine apostolical teaching in the New Testament, we have only to go back to that, and drink from the fountain itself, and not depend on the long and tortuous pipes that run through centuries of corruption and darkness, for the blessed water of life. This is what

Jesus and the Apostles have told us to do, and we are satisfied with their authority.

Hence if it were impossible to trace the historical connection of the Presbyterian Church further back than the Reformation, it would have precisely the same connection with the primitive Church that all other Protestant Churches have, and not a whit less of any authority that comes from that connection. And as, after all, the only authority which any Church possesses must come from Christ, we are satisfied when we reach that authority, without troubling ourselves with what Paul rightly called "fables and endless genealogies, which minister questions, rather than godly edifying, which is in faith."

But as some may lay stress on this connection, we propose to show that the Presbyterian Church, through the Church of Scotland, has through this ancient Church of the Culdees, a more unbroken historical connection with the primitive Church, than even the Anglican Church, and that if there is any value in this kind of succession at all, we have it. This we will attempt to do by maintaining a series of historical propositions leading to this conclusion.

CHAPTER III.

THE PLANTING OF CHRISTIANITY IN SCOTLAND.

Introduced near to, or during the Apostolic age, by Greek, not Roman Missionaries—Testimonials to the Oriental origin of Scottish Christianity—Appendix on the Greek element in Scotland.

IN tracing the historic relations of the Culdee Church, with the Apostolic Church on the one hand, and the Reformation Church on the other, we propose to show, that Christianity was introduced into Scotland at a very early day; probably near to, if not during the time of the Apostles; that it was then, and continued for many ages to be, essentially Presbyterian in doctrine and order; that when Popery was established in the 12th or 13th Century, it was the act of the government forcing it on the people; and hence, from the nature of the case, as well as from existing evidence, this enforced religion never succeeded in wholly rooting out the primitive Culdee faith from the popular heart; that when the Reformation came, it was the act of the people forcing it on the government, thus reversing the act which fastened Popery on them four hundred years before, and casting it off as an incubus; and that the Reformation Church of Scotland was, therefore, simply a reäppearance of this old primeval Church, which had been smothered, but not extinguished, during this occupancy of Popery; and that it is thus linked authentically by an unbroken, historic connection of faithful men with the very days of the Apostles. If these points can be fairly made out, it will be seen that we connect back with apostolic times, not through the Church of Rome, but independent of it; and that like the river Alphœus, which was said to take its rise far up in the mountains of Greece, to enter the Italian sea, passing under it and reäppearing in the beautiful fountain of Arethusa, so this stream that gushed out among the hills of Scotland can be traced back, under the troubled waves of Italian supremacy, to purer fountains far away among the primitive seats of the Gospel in the earlier Churches of the East. Our historical connection then will be not with Latin Christianity, but with the older and purer forms of it, found nearer its original seat in Jerusalem.) Of course we can only give brief hints of evidence on these points, as a statement of the whole would fill volumes.

The first proposition is, *that Christianity was introduced into Scotland very near to, if not during the lives of the Apostles.*

It must be remembered, that when Christianity was first preached, Britain was a Roman province, and so continued for 400 years. But the seat of

the Roman power was mainly in England. Owing
to the inaccessible mountains, and the warlike character of the Picts and Scots, Caledonia never was
subject to the Roman power, and in spite of repeated efforts to subdue these hardy tribes, Scotland remained unconquered to the very last. This
fact would make it a retreat for any one who desired
to escape from the power of Rome. Hence, as soon
as persecution began to rage in the empire, the
mountains of Scotland would offer an asylum so
inviting that this fact alone would drive persecuted
Christians to "flee to the mountains," where of
course they would tell to the wild tribes inhabiting
them, the story of the cross.

But there was another cause that would also lead
Christian missionaries there. Scotland was occupied
in part, at least, by a branch of the great Celtic
race, which taking its origin in Asia, extended its
migrations through Asia Minor, across to Northern
Italy and Southern Germany, to Gaul, Iberia, and
the British Isles, giving its indelible characteristics
to the Celtic people of France, Scotland, and Ireland to this day. A branch of this race occupied
Galatia, and it is very easy to see from the Epistle
to the Galatians, that these Gauls of ancient times
had precisely the characteristics of the Gauls of
modern times, and would be likely to act from the
same impulses. A moments reflection on these

impulses, will show, that the Celts of Galatia and other portions of the East, were not likely to possess the religion of Christ long, without communicating it to their Celtic brethren of the West. This was an easy thing by the ordinary channels of commercial intercourse, which were open through all parts of the Roman empire. Hence, we find the origin of that Celtic Christianity, which is as distinct a type of the Church, as the Greek, Latin, or Teutonic Christianity, the marked differences of which are familiar to every Christian scholar. It is a curious fact, illustrating the general object we have in view, that race makes itself known in religion as much as in civil affairs. Latin Christianity has always prevailed, and still does so among the races speaking the Latin tongues; whilst among Teutonic races and partly among Celtic, the Reformation supplanted it, as if it never could take a deep root in these races. But the main fact we insist on is, that the blood relationship of the Celtic tribes, would naturally lead to missionary efforts from the Celtic or Galatian Christians of the East among their brethren in the West, and that these efforts would be likely to extend to the Celtic tribes of Britain, Ireland and Scotland.

These facts will prepare us for the evidence bearing on the first introduction of Christianity into the British isles. There is much dispute about some of the authorities cited, but there is one about which there is no doubt. Tertullian, the Christian Cicero, who was born about sixty years after the death of John, the last of the Apostles, asserts that "those parts of Britain that were inaccessible to the Romans," (i. e. Scotland,) "had become subject to Christ."* Here then we find within less than a century of the death of John, that Scotland had so far received Christianity as to warrant Tertullian to say, that it was subject to Christ. It must have required a considerable time for such a result to be reached, among the hostile tribes of Caledonia, whose native religion was that ancient and powerful form of Paganism, the religion of the Druids. It must have required a great deal of labour to banish this old and terrible superstition so as to warrant the language of Tertullian. This general consideration would throw the earliest professors and teachers of Christianity back very near to the death of the Apostle John, if not before it.

This early date is favoured by the probabilities of a very early introduction of Christianity into Britain. Baronius, the great Romish historian of the Church, asserts on the authority of some manuscript, in the Vatican, that Christianity was carried to Britain A. D., 35. If so, this was several years previous to its being preached in Rome, and

* Adv. Jud. c. 7.

the missionaries must have come from Palestine direct, or Asia Minor. When it was once introduced into Britain, the wonderful missionary zeal of the Apostolical Church would soon lead men to carry it into Scotland, for there was no obstacle in the one case much more formidable than was found in the other. Hence, we may infer a very early date to the first introduction of Christianity into Scotland, one running back very near, and possibly much beyond, that of the death of John.

This is confirmed by the fact that the type of Christianity introduced was not that of Rome, but that of the Eastern Churches. Neander says, that "the peculiarity of the later British Church is evidence against its origin from Rome; for in many ritual matters it departed from the usage of the Romish Church, and agreed much more nearly with the Churches of Asia Minor. It withstood, for a long time, the authority of the Romish papacy. This circumstance would seem to indicate that the Britons had received their Christianity either immediately, or through Gaul, from Asia Minor, a thing quite possible and easy, by means of the commercial intercourse." * Dean Milman refers to the same fact in stating the struggle that afterwards occurred between the Scottish and Romish missionaries in England, (which we will recur to

* Ch. His., 1, 85.

again,) when he says, "it is curious to find Greek Christianity thus at the verge of the Romish world, maintaining some of its usages and coëquality." *

Hence, many of the most eminent scholars have reached the conclusion, which these facts certainly warrant, that the Christianity of Scotland was introduced directly from some of the Greek Churches of the East, and not from any Church having any connection with Rome. Thus Spotswood, the Scottish Historian says, "I verily think that under Domitian's persecutions, some of John's disciples first preached the Gospel in this kingdom. * * * Sure not long after the ascension of our Lord, at least when the Apostle St. John yet lived, the faith of Christ was known and embraced in divers places of this kingdom." † Buchanan, in his History of Scotland, concurs in this view, and says, that "the Scots were taught Christianity by the disciples of the Apostle John," and that many Christians of the Britons, fearing the cruelty of Domitian, took their journey into Scotland; of whom many, famous both in learning and integrity of life, stayed and fixed their habitation therein." ‡ The author of the Early Dawn of Christian Life in England, says, "history proves that the early British Church derived its

* Lat. Christianity, II, 196.
† Hist. Scotland, 1, 191.
‡ Lib. 4, 5.

faith and its customs from the Eastern Church."* A recent writer in the *British and Foreign Evangelical Review*, on the Church History of the Celts as a race, takes the same position, and says, "How hard it is to account for the fact that the peculiar Easter usages of the Churches of Asia Minor, were reproduced in the churches of Wales and Ireland and Scotland. But if, now, we bring into view the ascertained fact that the Christianized Celts of Galatia adhered to these usages, that no early missionaries could be so well qualified to diffuse the Gospel among the Celts of the West, as the converted Celts of the East, we become sensible of a highly augmented probability attaching to the ancient tradition of the British Churches, that the Gospel came to them in the first instance, not from Gaul, or from Rome, but from Asia Minor, after the Churches planted by St. Paul that there had fallen under the apostolical rule of St. John."†

These authorities, when we remember the Church relations of most of the authors, will probably be sufficient to establish several points, to every unprejudiced mind. First, that Christianity was introduced into Scotland very near to, if not during the lives of the later Apostles, partly by direct missionary effort, and partly by the stress of persecution, driving the primitive disciples to the moun-

* P. 26. † No. lvii., p. 534.

tains of Scotland as an asylum; secondly, that the first missionaries came from Asia Minor, and not from Italy, and brought with them the doctrines and usages of the Grecian Churches, and not the Church of Rome; and that hence the early Scottish Church and all other Churches lineally descended from it, were as independent of the Romish Church in their origin, as the Greek, Coptic, or any other distinct Church now, or formerly in existence. If then we can show that this primitive Scottish faith never wholly died out in Scotland, but lived on during the usurpation of Popery, and reäppeared in the Reformation Church, we will have shown that our present Presbyterian Church traces its lineage backward to the Churches planted and watered by Paul and his associates, and then ministered to by John; a paternity with which the most fastidious lover of antiquity in ecclesiastical genealogy ought to be more than satisfied.

As the foregoing is a point of some importance, the following essay, called out by the original publication of this argument, and evidently written by a scholar, may be suitably appended to this chapter:

"THE GREEK ELEMENT IN SCOTLAND.

I have been much interested in those well written articles upon the Culdee Church. The writer has fully made out his case, and proved both the antiquity of this Church, and also its Presbyterian character.

I wish to call attention to one fact that seems to have been overlooked, and which goes to show the intimate connexion that must have existed between the Scottish nation and the Greeks in very ancient times.

We find Greek names common in Scotland, from a very early period, especially among the Highlanders, who represent the ancient Celtic race which formerly peopled that land. The name Alexander is very common; so common that its abbreviation into Alec, Sandy, or Sawney, is used to designate a man of Scotland.

Constantine is frequently found among the list of old Scottish kings; while Hector, in its Highland form of Eachin, is and has been a very common name among this people.

The national name in Scotland, is a Greek word Andrew; it means a man. St. Andrew was the patron saint of the nation. St. Andrew's was at once the seat and name of the chief University and of the chief Bishopric. The cross on which the Holy Apostle was crucified bore the form of the letter X; it is still called St. Andrew's cross, and is borne as a part of the coat-of-arms of the Scottish nation. Now this form or letter is nothing more or less, than the initial letter of the Greek word Christos, or The Christ.

The symbol of the Scottish people is, therefore, the Greek letter which stands for the very name of our Lord.   Now these things are not of recent adoption; they are found among the very earliest records of the nation, and moreover they are so common as to characterize the people.

Other names and other points of resemblance might be traced if time and space permitted.   I merely call attention to this peculiarity, and will make, in explanation of it, a few remarks.

There was no commerce, there were no colonies, and there was no other connection that we have been able to discover between Greece and Scotland. And not only was there no communication, but even where the Greeks traded or colonized, they did not impress their names on the native races.   And that these names are not Celtic or developed from the Celtic, we find in the fact that they do not appear in any other country inhabited by Celts and visited by Greeks; they are not found in France, in Ireland, or in Cornwall.

There were two points in which the Celt and Greek came in contact; one was the old Greek colony of Marseilles, in the south of France, and the other was the coast of Cornwall, where the Greek merchants came for tin. The Celts having no writ-

4

ing of their own, adopted the letters of the Greek alphabet, and used them in writing their own language. Of course all of them who had any intercourse with these Greek traders, learned in time, a smattering of that language.

Another thing tended to bring Gaul and Greek in contact. Many years before our era, a nation of Gauls had marched, plundering through the world, until they had finally settled in Galatia, in Asia Minor. There they were mingled with the Greeks. And they kept up intercourse with the other Celts of Europe through Marseilles, and also over land.

It was to these Celts of Asia, that Paul wrote his Epistle to the Galatians. It was the first written of all his Epistles, and I doubt not was used by them in spreading a knowledge of the Gospel among other Celtic tribes. Paul, led by the Holy Spirit, preached to this outlying post of the Celtic race, and from them came forth the missionaries who spread the knowledge wherever the Celtic tongue was spoken.

I think it more than probable that Christianity, having Greek, or Greek speaking Celts, as missionaries, entered Gaul through Marseilles, and Britain through Cornwall. About Marseilles, in Southern France, we find long after the much persecuted Albigenses, the remains of the old Gaulish churches.

And in the mountain valleys, at the sources of the Rhone, yet remain the Churches of the Waldenses. I have no doubt that these Churches derived their origin through Marseilles, from the preaching of Celtic Greeks from Asia.

From Cornwall may have emanated, by similar means, those Christian Churches of Wales and England, as well as those planted across the sea in Ireland, where the persecuted went as to a place of refuge. The early Disciples obeyed the command, " If they persecute you in one city, flee ye to another, and as ye go preach."

All the preachers of that early day, if they were not Greek, at least spoke and taught in that language. Indeed the Old Testament had been translated into Greek, while the Gospels and Epistles were all written in that language, even the Epistle to the Galatians, the only one not addressed to a Greek community. The Church of early times was in language a Greek Church.

How then did these names become so common in Scotland? By Greek missionaries preaching among the people. To name a child after a pastor is common in all religious communities. And the very fact therefore that we find these Greek names common in Scotland, when there could have been no other point of connexion than that of religion, leads to the conclusion that Greek Christians had penetrated at an early period into that land, had settled among the people and converted them to the true faith, and that their names were adopted among the tribes of Scotland as the national ones. They must have been numerous and thoroughly spread among the people; a few isolated missionaries could not have caused this national peculiarity.

I believe that this faith was taught very early in the Christian era to the natives of Brittan, and that one important means of accomplishing this result in so remote a place as Brittan rather than in Gaul, or Spain, or Germany was this, that about the time when Christianity began to spread over the world, the Roman armies were invading Brittan.

Ten years after our Lord's death, the first invasion began; and forty years after that death, the Roman had marched into South Scotland and reached the Grampian Hills. Wherever the Roman conquered, he inhabited.

Now these armies were marched from the East to this conquest. It is probable that among the soldiers there may have been Christians, and certain that the teachers of this religion may have been among those who formed the immigrating population who followed the army and settled the country.

When persecution arose in the land, the converts and their pastors would fly northward into the wilds of the mountains and lakes. Each persecution would add to their number until these fugitives, coalescing with the native tribes, would make this religion that of the people.

We have historic proof that immense numbers of Saxons fled into Scotland from the Normans, and doubtless similar escapings took place when the Romans invaded Brittan, and when the Saxons afterwards slaughtered the Romanized Celts.

From these various wars and invasions, I doubt not, came the Churches of Wales, Scotland, and of Ireland."

CHAPTER IV.

CULDEE PRESBYTERIANISM.

Scottish Church older than English—Struggle with Roman Missionaries for foothold in Eng'and—Anglican Testimony to these facts—
Doctrines and Polity of the Culdee Church substantially identical with those of Modern Presbyterian Churches—Testimony of
Historians.

HAVING shown in a previous chapter that Christianity was introduced into Scotland very near to,
if not during the lives of the Apostles, we now
propose to show, *that this primitive form of Christianity, as we find it in the Culdee Church, was
substantially identical with that of the Reformed
Church of Scotland.*

We do not, of course mean to affirm a minute
identity in the faith and forms of the Culdee
Church and the present Presbyterian Church, or
that every feature of that early Church was wise
and scriptural; for this would be impossible, in
churches whose outward surroundings were so
entirely different. Even now, there are features in
the Church system in a heathen country, different
from those in a Christian; in a time of war, from a
time of peace; and it ought to be so in that religion which became "all things to all men, that by
all means it might save some." What we do affirm,

is that in this **Culdee** Church there was no Popery and no prelacy, that in its main features of doctrine and **order, it** was, as far as we can ascertain its peculiarities, Presbyterian, governed **by** Presbyters.

In tracing the history of **this early** Scottish Church, it will **be** remembered **that when it** was first established, Britain was **a province of** Rome, **and** continued **to be** until **the** evacuation of the island by the Romans, A. D., 420, when **the** disunion and anarchy which ensued, invited the predatory incursions of **the Picts and Scots.** To resist **these** formidable invaders, Vortigern, **A. D.,** 449, invited the Saxons **to** come and aid him, who, under the leadership **of** Hengist **and** Horsa, **soon seized** the **country** they came **to** protect, slaughtered **the** Britons, and drove the miserable remnant that escaped the sword, **to** the mountains of Wales and some **of** the more inaccessible islands. The Saxons, being Pagans, destroyed the Christianity **that** since the reign **of** Constantine had flourished **in** England, and restored the dark superstitions **of the** Druidic religion. For a century **and a** half this Pagan rule prevailed in England. But in Scotland, Ireland **and** Wales, it was otherwise. Scotland, **never** having been conquered **by the Saxons,** any **more** than by the Romans, **retained her** primitive faith, and with Ireland, enjoyed the light of a pure Christianity, while England was covered with the gloom of Paganism.

It was during this period of Saxon heathenism that the celebrated incident occurred which determined the religious history of England, by attracting to it the attention of the Church of Rome, which we may as well transcribe, as it is one of those pebbles in the fountain that determine the channel of the future river. When Gregory the Great was a simple monk of St. Andrew, he saw some beautiful, faired-haired boys exposed for sale in the market-place of Rome. He inquired from whence they came. "From Britain." "Are they Christians?" "They are still pagans." "Alas! that the Prince of Darkness should possess forms of such loveliness! That such beauty of countenance should want the better beauty of soul!" He asked of what nation they were. "Angles," was the reply. "Truly," he said, "they are angels! From what province?" "That of Deira." "Truly, they must be rescued *de ira*, (from the wrath of God.") "What is the name of their King?" "Ælla." "Yea," said Gregory, "Allelulia must be sung in the dominions of that King."*

From that hour he resolved that England shou'd be converted, that he would become a Christian Cæsar and re-conquer it to Rome; and although his desire

*II. Milman, p. 48.

was frustrated at that time, he carried it out when he ascended the pontifical throne. This little incident was the occasion of linking England to Rome, rather than to Scotland in its ecclesiastical relations, as we shall see, and thus changing the whole current of Church history as far as it is affected by the Anglican Church.

During this reign of Saxon Paganism, Christianity continued to exist and grow in Scotland and Ireland, and so closely were these countries connected ecclesiastically, that they are both called by ancient writers Scotia, and their inhabitants Scots. This probably had its origin in the fact that it was the Celtic tribes in both that were Christianized, and they were regarded as one people, although living in separate islands, and constituted substantially one Church. And it is a curious fact that the patron saint of Ireland was a Scotsman, while the patron saint of Scotland was an Irishman. St. Patrick or Patricius, the son of a Scottish deacon of Roman blood, indeed a patrician, as his name indicates, was a very successful missionary in Ireland, but not the introducer of Christianity there. It had been in existence several centuries before, and produced some eminent men in the history of the Church long before St. Patrick was born. Columba, the man who has given Iona so much of its lustre, was an Irishman, of noble, indeed royal lineage, being of the family of the Kings of Ulster, and related to a royal family in Scotland. The probabilities seem to be, that at that time Christianity had a stronger foothold among the Scots than it had among the Picts, and that Columba desired to convert the Pictish tribes to Christianity, and for this purpose determined to make a lodgement on some place that would be accessible to both countries. For this purpose he selected the sacred isle of Iona, then the seat of a Druidic College; and A. D., 564, landed there with twelve companions to found a Christian College, which should send forth missionaries to all parts of the heathen world. He was bitterly opposed by the Druids, but succeeded in getting possession of the Island by a grant from its royal owner, a Pictish king. Here then he founded that memorable College, which for centuries was a source of light to Northern Europe, by sending forth missionaries properly trained for their work. When this College is called a monastery, the name is calculated to mislead, unless the difference between it and other institutions called by that name is remembered. The monasteries connected with Iona were as different from the monastic institutions of Benedict, Francis or Dominic, as the celibate fellowships of an English university are from an Italian or Spanish monastery. Indeed they

differed more; for the monks of Iona were allowed
to marry and often were married, while the fellow
of an English university forfeits his fellowship by
marriage. Their wives were not allowed to reside
in the monastery; but their family establishments
were kept up, and some of the offices and titles to
property were hereditary. We have not room to
describe these differences in detail, but it is
sufficient to say that the whole designs of the
two were radically different. The institutions
of Iona were not designed to cultivate eremites
and solitary ascetics, but to train Christian
scholars and missionaries, who would go forth as
soldiers of Christ, trained to conquer and occupy
the outlying territory of heathenism. This it did
to an extent that is amazing, and only now beginning to be understood by the laborious researches
of German scholars, who show that this Scottish
Church did more to carry a *pure* Gospel to all
parts of Great Britain, France, Germany and
Switzerland, during the 6th, and 7th, and 8th centuries than all Christendom besides, and with this
Gospel, to diffuse letters and science, industry and
civilization.

They were called Culdees, a name of doubtful
etymology, but imposed on them like Huguenots and
Methodists, &c., from some fact in their character,

connected with their separation from the world and their consecration to God.

It is a curious fact, not generally known, that it is to this Culdee Church that England owes some of the first efforts to Christianize her people, after the Saxons had restored Paganism there; and so far is it from being true that the English Church has higher claims to antiquity than the Scottish Church, it is the simple truth of history that the latter carried Christianity into England when it was in Saxon Paganism, and had they been allowed to continue their labours, the whole history of the Anglican Church would have been changed, and hence, if the claim of mother Church is to be allowed to either, it belongs to the Church of Scotland. These missionary labours arose on this wise.

During the stormy years of the Saxon Heptarchy, (which Milton compares to skirmishes of kites and crows,) royal families were often banished for a time, and had to seek a refuge in adjacent countries. In one of these banishments, Oswald, King of Northumbria, found an asylum in Iona, and was educated there during his stay. On his recovery of the throne, he desired to introduce among his own people, the superior forms of religion and science he had seen in Iona, and accordingly sent for Culdee missionaries, who laboured for some time among the Saxons with no little success. Had they been allowed to continue, England would have been Culdeised, and her history changed. But several facts turned the scale of events. One of these was the mission of Augustine (not the great Augustine) to bring England over to Rome. When Gregory became Pope, he remembered the vow he had made, and sent a deputation to convert England, which after labouring for a time in the south of England, met these Culdee labourers at work in the North. The radical difference between the Culdee faith and the Romish, is shown by the fact that they could not labour together, and that the Romish missionaries found that the expulsion of the Culdees was necessary to their success. Milman, in his "Latin Christianity," speaking of this collision, says, "One half of the island had been converted by the monks from Scotland, the other by those from Rome. They were opposed on certain points of discipline, held hardly of less importance than vital truths of the Gospel."* In describing the debate on these points at the Synod of Whitby, Milman refers to the claim of the Scottish Missionaries, that they held an uninterrupted descent of their tradition from St. John, whilst the Romans pleaded the authority of St. Peter, and the King finally sided with the repre-

*II. 196.

sentatives of Rome, and the Culdees were compelled to retire to Scotland. Neander, also, in referring to this struggle, says, that when it occurred, "it became necessary for men to decide between the Roman and the Scottish Church influences; and the manner in which this decision was made could not fail to be attended with the most important effects on the shaping of ecclesiastic relations over all England; for had the Scottish tendency prevailed, England would have obtained a more free Church constitution, and a reäction against the Romish hierarchical system would have continued to go forth from this quarter."* Although the Culdees were banished from England, the controversy continued for several centuries. At a Synod held in Northampton, A. D. 1716, Gilbert Murray, a Scotsman, resisted the claims of the English Church, and said in his speech, that " her mother, the Church of Scotland, which from the beginning hath been Catholic and free," ought not to yield; and reminded the English, how by means of this ancient Church, England had been brought, "when straying in the wilderness of heathenism into the safeguard of true faith and way unto life, even unto Jesus Christ the Author of eternal rest;" and concluded his bold and masterly effort by declaring, that

*Ch. Hist. III. 24.

although he should stand alone, he would dissent "from subjecting the free Church of his fathers to any other power than that of the Lord, unto whom immediately she was subject; and if it were needful to die in this cause, declaring his readiness to lay down his neck unto the sword."* The tone of this manly speech reminds one of later times, and shows that the spirit of the fearless Murray was exactly the same with his spiritual descendants Knox, Henderson, and Chalmers, and that their metal has the same true ring. The fact then is one that cannot be doubted, that the Church of Scotland and the Church of Rome struggled for the occupancy of England, and hence that the Anglican Church, which was the result of that struggle, is a younger Church than that of Scotland.

A striking testimony of this is given by a learned clergyman of the Church of England of the 17th century, Mr. T. Jones, naval chaplain to the Duke of York, (afterwards James II.,) in a curious volume published by him to show "the historical title of the British Church, and by what ministry the Gospel was first planted in England." Having been written before the rise of the modern High Church spirit, it gives the testimony of a very earnest Episcopalian, who distinctly affirms that

*Alexander's Iona, p. 107.

Presbyterians are "schismatics," but does not deny them a Church existence. We quote a few sentences from his learned work. He says:—"And first it is to be remembered and repeated that the Gospel from its first planting by the Apostles was never extinguished or eradicated from among the Brittains, (i. e. the Celts or aboriginal inhabitants of the British islands,) as it soon fared with our Augustine's adventures upon the English, but that they persevered to praise God *to this day*, in the same Religion and Language with their forefathers, the 1600 years and upwards, as they trust to continue till Christ's second coming; being the same religion that was alike preserved among the Cornish * * * and *over all Scotland and Ireland*, * * * where it is clear against all the arts and inventions, * * * that the first planting of the faith among the people was by the Brittish (Celtic), and not by Romish Ministry."* He then mentions the same fact that we have elsewhere noted, that these British Churches, of which the Scotch was one, received the Gospel from Asia Minor, and not from Western Europe, and traced their maternity not to Rome, but to the mother Church of Jerusalem.† He also states the facts above recited as to the Scottish missions to Saxon England, as

*P. 231.   †p. 233.

follows,* "But Oswald and his companions, during his Exile in Scotland, were Baptized and
brought up in the Christian Religion, according
to the Brittish (Celtic) Institution, as it differed
from the Roman, and being settled on his Throne
by Cadwallian, sent to Scotland for Doctors to
Convert the remainder of his Subjects; to that
end Aidanus and Finnan and Diuma are sent, who
were Monkes of a Brittish isle belonging to the
Picts (Iona) who bestowed the same on St. Col-
umbanus (Columba) who built a monastery there
* * where the Abbot was Superior to all the
Clergy of those parts and to the *Bishop himself*,
and the Rites and Customs of the Brittains were
most strictly observed and kept to the last."
When it is remembered that the Abbot or Presi-
dent of the College of Iona was a simple Elder,
it is plain that Prelacy was not a part of those
"Rites and Customs," for we have here a Presbyter ranking a Bishop in authority.

Of this mission of Aidan, he says,† that he
and "Holy King Oswald, were the Chief Authors
and Instruments under God of the Conversion of
the English to the Christian Faith over all the
Land, not only in Northumberland, where they
Reigned and resided, but over the rest of the
English Heptarchies." Again‡ he speaks of

*p. 266.   †p. 269.   ‡p. 390.

"the Ancient, Apostolick, Brittish Faith, which the Scotch and Irish defended with us heretofore against Monk Augustine and planted among the English, before he and his Successors sowed their Tares among them."*

Here then we have the candid testimony of a learned clergyman of the Church of England, that "the Conversion of the English over all the Land," was due to the Culdee missionaries of the Scottish Church, an admission which only the truth could have extorted from the Royal Chaplain of the Duke of York. Hence unless the child can be older than its mother, it must follow that the Anglican Church cannot claim as high an antiquity as the Scottish, and that those who trace their orders to that Church, have certainly no right to contend for an Apostolical source any better, if as good, as those who derive their succession from the Church of Scotland.

We now inquire what were the doctrines of this Culdee Church? The facts already cited, prove that they were not Romish, but so antagonistic as to be incapable of coëxisting with those of Rome. Whether they were Prelatic, or Presbyterian, is a point that has been disputed, and it may be sufficient to give the conclusions to which learned men in the English and other Churches

* Jones's Rome, No Mother Church to England, London, 1679

have come, who could not be thought to be affected by sectarian prejudice. The evidence is too voluminous to be condensed into the brief space left us, and we must content ourselves with giving the opinions of competent witnesses who have examined it in the original authorities.

That there were bishops in the old Culdee Church is true, but it is equally true that these bishops were not prelates, claimed and exercised no authority over other presbyters, in a word were, Presbyterian, not Prelatic bishops. This fact is clear from many witnesses. Thus Archbishop Usher admits that the Church government of the churches founded by St. Patrick was parochial, not diocesan Episcopacy. He says, " We read in Nennius that at the beginning, St. Patrick founded 365 churches, and ordained 365 bishops, and 3,000 presbyters or elders." Here then was a bishop and about twelve elders to each church, which is Presbyterianism, and as St. Patrick probably borrowed his system from that of his native country, we see what the Church order of Scotland was at that time. This is further conceded by the learned prelate in the admission, that Palladius was sent in the 5th century to be the first (prelatic) bishop of the Scottish Church, and if the first, he had no predecessors. His mission failed, however, as he died soon after his arrival in Scotland.

Bishop Stillingfleet, in his Irenicum, ch. 7, sec. 6, states, "Some whole nations seem to have been without any bishops at all, if we may believe their own historians. So if we may believe the great antiquaries of the Church of Scotland, that Church was governed by their Culdei, as they called their presbyters, without any bishop over them, for a long time. Johannes Major says, "the Scots were instructed in the faith without bishops, by the priests and monks," but lest that should be interpreted only of their conversion, Johannes Fordonus is clear and full to their government from the time of their conversion A. D. 263, to the coming of Palladius A. D. 430, that they were "governed by presbyters and monks only, following the order of the Primitive Church."

The Pictorial History of England, a work of great ability and impartiality, says,* "Much controversy has been waged upon the nature of the system of ecclesiastical polity founded by Columba; one class of writers, at the head of whom, is the acute and learned Selden, maintaining it to have been strictly Presbyterian, while others contend that the Culdees, as the clergy generally were called, were subject to Episcopal authority. The former is the opinion that has been more generally held, and that seems

*Vol. I, p. 218.

most conformable to the expressions of Bede,* the earliest authority on the subject. The small and barren island of Iona, after this, soon became illustrious in the labours and triumphs of the Christian Church, and the Culdees, animated with the zeal of their founder, not only devoted their efforts to enlighten their own country, but became adventurous missionaries to fields the most dangerous and remote. It is gratifying also to observe that with all the disputations as to their form of Church government, there is a general agreement as to the purity and simplicity both of their doctrines and lives. Even Bede, though indignant at their rejection of the authority of the Roman bishop, testifies, that "they preached only such works of charity and piety as they could learn from the prophetical, evangelical, and apostolical writings." Of the care with which they were trained to be the guardians of learning and instructors of the people, we may form some idea from the fact that eighteen years of study were frequently required of them before they were ordained." On p. 233, it is also said, "the English writers of that age, nevertheless, bear testimony to the purity of their lives, and the zeal of their apostolical labors, while they denounce their exclusive devotedness to the authority of Scrip-

Hist. Ecc., lib. III, c. 4.

ture, their rejection of Romish ceremonies, doctrines and traditions, the nakedness of their forms of worship, and the republican character of their ecclesiastical government." D'Aubigne says, "Iona, governed by a simple elder, had become a missionary College. It has been sometimes called a monastery, but the dwelling of the grand-son of Fergus (Columba) in nowise resembled the Popish convents. When its youthful inmates desired to spread the knowledge of Jesus Christ, they thought not of going elsewhere for Episcopal ordination. Kneeling in the chapel of Icolmkill, they were set apart by the laying on of the hands of the *Elders;* they were called Bishops, but remained obedient to the *Elder* or presbyter of Iona. They even consecrated other Bishops; thus Finan laid hands upon Diuma, Bishop of Middlesex. The British Christians attached great importance to the ministry, but not to one form in preference to another. Presbytery and Episcopacy were with them, as in the Primitive Church, almost identical."* Prof. Ebrard, of Germany, one of the latest and most learned investigators of this field, in his recent book on the Culdee Church, after thoroughly sifting the testimony, comes to this conclusion, " The true explanation of the fact is this: By ordination, a man became a presbyter, a presbyterate was the sacred office, the sacerdotal order. A presbyter who presided over a monastery, was the abbot or father of that monastery. But in cases where a monastery, by missionary labour, succeeded in forming congregations of Christian converts in the surrounding country, the spiritual oversight of these congregations was undertaken either by the abbot himself or by some other of the presbyters, who was named to that office. The holder of this office was called a bishop."* This is precisely the doctrine of the Presbyterian Church in her present standards.

Mr. Jamieson, in his History of the Culdees, says, "After the most impartial investigation of this subject of which I am capable, I have not found a shadow of proof, that any of those sent forth as bishops from that island, were ordained by such as claimed a dignity superior to that of presbyter." Michelet says, "the Culdees recognized hardly more of the hierarchical state than the modern Scotch Presbyterians." Many other testimonies might be added to these, but they will suffice to prove the proposition which we laid down, that the early Culdee Church, was in its Church government and doctrines not Popish and Prelatic, but essentially Presbyterian, and in the language with which Ebrard sums up his exhaustive investigations of its doctrines, "Evangelical, not only because it was free and independent of Rome, and when the Papal Church came into contact with it, always and obstinately repudiated its authority under appeal to the single and supreme authority of Holy Scripture, but above all, because in its inner life, it was penetrated throughout by the main principles of the Evangelical Church." In its government and ordination by presbyters alone, in its evangelical doctrines, in its missionary spirit, in its sturdy independence, in its jealousy of the crown rights of Jesus, in its attention to learning and multiplication of schools, and other particulars, it is substantially identical with the modern Presbyterian Church.

CHAPTER V.

REIGN OF POPERY IN SCOTLAND.

Struggle between the Church of Rome and the old Church of Scotland—The Culdee Church "cast down, but not destroyed"—Improbability of such a destruction—Proof of its existence during the Romish Usurpation.

HAVING given evidence to prove that Christianity was planted in Scotland very near to, if not during the lives of the Apostles, and from an Asiatic and not a European source, from the Churches ministered to by Paul and John, and not the Church of Rome; and that this primitive Church of the Culdees, was not Popish or Prelatic, but essentially Presbyterian, actuated by the same spirit, and holding substantially the same doctrines and order with the Reformation Church of Scotland, we wish now to trace its existence during the reign of Popery in Scotland, and to show, that there is good reason to believe that this old primeval faith never died out among the people of Scotland, and that this fact alone can explain the peculiarities of their history. We have traced this primitive Presbyterian Church down to the date of its contact with Popery in England, whence it was expelled by force, only to renew the contest in Scotland, where Popery sought to make further aggressions, and after a long and bitter struggle, succeeded in suppressing for the time, the old Culdee Church.

Our next proposition then is, *that when Popery was established as the recognized religion of Scotland, it was the forcible act of the government, and not the voluntary act of the people.*

There is something exceedingly interesting in the gallant struggle of this old Culdee Church, with the gigantic power of Rome, continuing as it did for nearly five hundred years. The particulars of the struggle are too numerous to detail in our brief space, and we can only state the general facts, referring for the authorities on which these statements are made, to the elaborate works of such standard writers as McLauchlan, Jamieson, Ebrard and others, who give them in full.

We have noted the first struggle of Culdeeism with Rome about A. D. 650. It continued until establishment of Popery by David I. in A. D. 1150, and indeed for some time afterwards, for the final overthrow did not take place until the suppression of the Culdees of St. Andrews, A. D. 1297. Alexander says,* " As Romish influence advanced it became necessary to silence the continual protest which these men (the Culdees)

* Iona, p. 118.

maintained against the doctrines and pretensions of the Romish Church; and for this purpose, all those means by which a religious body may be annihilated, were systematically resorted to. By corrupting those who could be tempted by the bribe of ecclesiastical rank and wealth, by expelling from their monasteries those who obstinately adhered to the belief and practice of their fathers, by vexatious and iniquitous law suits, by dazzling the eyes of the people with a more splendid ritual than that followed by the simple presbyters of the Columba order, by calumniating their character, and affecting a superiour standard of morals,—in short, by all the means by which an adroit, determined, and unscrupulous party may enfeeble the influence and paralyze the resolution of a sect it had resolved to destroy, did the adherents of the Romish Church labour to sweep from the land all vestiges of the Culdees. It was not, however, until the thirteenth century that they entirely succeeded, and even then they only suppressed the Colleges of the Culdees and dispersed their members. The latter still continued to labour as individuals, and in many remote parts of the country, kept alive the flame of pure Christianity, long after the whole land seemed to have sunk under Papal darkness, so that, to use

the words of Dr. Smith,* ' the reign of terror in
these lands was very short, and the darkness of
its night was intermixed with the light of many
stars.' "

The mere efforts of ecclesiastics would probably never have succeeded in suppressing this tough
old Church. It was done at the last by Scoto-
Saxon kings, and by English influence. Malcolm
Canmore, who ascended the Scottish throne in
A. D. 1058, married Margaret, the daughter of
William the Conqueror, a religious zealot, who
would probably have been an abbess had she
not been a queen. She determined to do for
the Scottish Church, what her father had done
for the English people, and as her husband had
been educated in England, she found no difficulty
in using him in her proselyting efforts. She pro-
ceeded with great craft and perseverance, con-
cealing her real object from the people, and professing only to desire a reform in some subordinate
matters. She succeeded in persuading the people
to make some changes. No effort was made to
introduce Prelacy, until after her death, A. D.
1093, when her sons determined to establish it.
In doing this, it is a suggestive fact mentioned by
McLauchlan,† that "with the exception of one or
two of the earlier and less prominent bishops of

*Life of Columba, p. 163.   † P. 418.

somewhat doubtful identity, we do not find one
native Scot, accepting, or being received into the
newly constituted offices.   Bishops and monks are
almost all importations from abroad ; some from
England, and others from France.   The whole
Romish system was to be introduced into Scotland, and the men who had to organize it, had to
be introduced with it."   The suddenness of the
establishment of the Scottish hierarchy shows that
it was done by force, and not by persuasion.
Every diocese in Scotland but one, was founded
between A. D. 1100 and A. D. 1153 ; the splendid
abbeys, whose ruins are all over Scotland, were
built at that time, hordes of foreign monks were
introduced and planted all over the land, and the
strong arm of royal power was wielded to crush
the Culdees.   What could these poor Culdee
presbyters do against such an army of monks and
prelates, backed by the army of the King and the
powerful influence of England ?   They were at
last driven out of their colleges, the last one being the Culdee institute of St. Andrews, which
was suppressed A. D. 1297, for resisting the
claims of the prelate of that see.   From this date
the old Culdee Church, as a visible organization,
disappears after one of the noblest and bravest
struggles in all history, a struggle running through
from five to seven centuries, in which every inch

of ground was disputed with the tenacity of a Thermopylæ, and given up at last because they were overpowered, not conquered.

Now we put it to any one who knows the working of human nature, whether it is likely that this old, unconquered faith that had battled for a thousand years, first against Paganism, and then against Popery, was likely to become extinct before a foreign religion, imposed upon a reluctant people by the sword? That foreign faith was not only to them an unscriptural one, but the faith of their enemies; the religion of Rome, to whose yoke their brave forefathers had never bowed when Rome was mightiest; the religion of England, that had never ceased to endeavour to bring Scotland into subjection, and never ceased to meet a stern defiance that chose death to subjugation. Was it likely that they would ever all submit to this foreign religion? Was it likely that the national spirit which shrined Wallace and Bruce in its heart of hearts, and flamed out so grandly on such bloody fields as that of Bannockburn, would ever cordially receive a religion forced on them by English rulers and English prelates? Surely it requires but a small knowledge of the ineradicable laws of human nature to infer, that a religious conquest of that kind never could wholly supplant the old religion in the hearts of the people, except by exterminating them, as was not done, in the case of the Scottish people. No religion ever has been destroyed by persecution, if the people professing it were not destroyed. Suppose in our country, the government were to force a religion upon us by the bayonet, would it ever take a deep root? We might submit to it, because we could not resist it; but would we love it? Would we adopt it in our hearts? Would we not continue to cherish the old and persecuted faith of our fathers in our very inmost heart, with a fidelity all the more undying because of this persecution? Would not that proscribed religion retire to the inaccessible fastnesses of the mountains, and there look and long for its day of deliverance? Would not its kindling memories of heroic endeavour and cruel persecution be whispered from sire to son, until its very sufferings would become hallowed, and the blood of its martyrs would be the seed of its Church? Then why should it not have been so with this old, invincible religion of the Culdees? Why should the Scottish people be less tenacious of their ancestral faith than we would be of ours? Have they from the very earliest times been a fickle people, given to change, and capable of being moulded in the way thus described?

Hence were there not a particle of evidence as

to the continued existence of the ancient Culdee
faith in the rural and mountainous districts of
Scotland during the occupation of Popery, we
would infer the fact from these unchangeable laws
of human nature, which are certainly not weaker
amongst the Scotch than amongst other races.
But we are not wholly without evidence on this
point. That evidence must be imperfect, for in
an age when there was no printing, no free intercourse between the Highlands and Lowlands, fre-
quent feuds and civil wars, and where the avowal
of Culdee sentiments would certainly expose to
persecution, we cannot expect any fulness of testimony as to the existence of sentiments which the
instinct of self-preservation would lead men to
conceal, and the profession of which could issue
in no useful result. The same persecution which
tended to perpetuate the hidden faith, would also
prevent the record of any evidence of its secret
existence. But that it did exist is the conclusion
of the ablest scholars who have looked into the
history of that period of darkness and confusion.
There were Reformers before the Reformation in
nearly every other country in Europe, and it was
passing strange if they did not exist in that country where the last and longest protest against
Romish usurpation existed; in the country where
the pure and primitive faith of the Apostolic

Church had maintained an unconquered existence for nearly a thousand years. That such witnesses for the truth did exist in Scotland, the continuation of the old Culdee Church, is the testimony of the most impartial judges.

In the History of the Lollards, published by the Religious Tract Society of London, a body which it would be ridiculous to suspect of Presbyterian predilections, or of sectarian bias of any kind, we have the following statements.* "In Scotland, as well as in England, the glad tidings of salvation through Christ Jesus were made known by the Apostles, or more probably by their immediate disciples." Then follows an account of the early Scottish Church precisely as we have given it from other sources, and need not therefore be repeated. After reciting the struggle with Popery in England, already described, it is added,† "In England, the Romanists speedily prevailed; but their encroachments, which included several other points, were more firmly resisted in Scotland; many left the North of England, where they were settled and took refuge among their Scottish neighbors, rather than give way to such proceedings." Matters went on from bad to worse, till at length, by degrees, in Scotland, as in other countries, "darkness covered the land, and gross darkness the people." A number, however, still were found who refused to bow their knees to the Baal of Romish superstition and power. Pope John XXII., in his bull for anointing King Robert Bruce, A. D. 1324, complained that there were many heretics in Scotland. Some, as Alcuin and others, resisted the doctrine of transubstantiation, and the Popish errors in general, and were declared heretics after their decease." * * * "The scattered remnant of the flock of Christ was then subjected to persecution. Historians do not furnish the full particulars, but that such a people existed, is clear from the evidence even of Popish writers, who, in their account of the Waldenses, relate, that individuals in that sect, and followers of Wickliff, were found in Scotland, as well as in England, doubtless they experienced similar treatment." After an account of the martyrdom of James Risby, A. D. 1422, and Paul Craw, A. D. 1431, for holding these doctrines, it is added,* "The romantic mountains and valleys of Scotland, however, afforded shelter to a scattered remnant of God's heritage. In their glens, as well as in the valleys of Piedmont, small assemblies were found, who looked to Christ Jesus as the only Mediator between God and man. In the year 1494, thirty persons called "The Lollards of

*P 337.

Kyle," a district of Ayrshire, were accused of various heresies before the King, and his council, by Blacater, Archbishop of Glasgow." The names and doctrines of these persons are then given, from which their identity with the Culdee Church of other days is very clear, after which the history is carried on to the establishment of the Reformation in A. D. 1550.

Hetherington, in his History of the Church of Scotland, * gives the facts at some length, and states as the conclusion to be drawn from them, that "Popery had not been able wholly to exterminate the purer faith and simpler system of the ancient Culdees, especially in Ayrshire, and perhaps also in Fife—the districts adjacent to St. Andrews and Iona,—the earliest abodes and the latest retreats of primitive Christianity in Scotland," * * * and that, "the doctrine of the Culdees continued to survive long after the suppression of their forms of Church Government."†

McLauchlan, the latest and perhaps ablest historian of the Culdee Church, states as the conclusion of the whole investigation so exhaustively set forth in his pages, "It requires but little acquaintance with Scottish history to observe that the principles of the old Culdee Church never were eradicated; that during the reign of the

Roman Church in the kingdom, they continued to exist, exhibiting themselves occasionally in such outbreaks as the letter of King Robert Bruce and his nobles to Pope John, on the uprising of the Lollards of Kyle, and finally culminating in the events of the Scottish Reformation. Those principles had regard, above all things, to the independence of the ancient Scottish kingdom and Church. They exist still fresh and vigorous as ever in the Scottish mind; nor is it easy to say for how much of what now distinguishes Scotland ecclesiastically, she is indebted to the ancient Culdee Church. One thing is plain, that notwithstanding the claims of the Church of Rome and its hierarchical organizations, to antiquity in Scotland, she can only claim four hundred of the eighteen hundred years that have elapsed since the planting of Christianity in the kingdom, viz: the period between A. D. 1150, when David established her, and A. D. 1550 when his establishment was overthrown by the resuscitation of the old Scottish principles at the Reformation." *

Alexander, Jamieson, and other historians, make similar statements, but these will probably suffice to show, that the ancient Culdee faith, after its long and gallant struggle with Rome, did not cease to exist, but, after the throne had forced

* P. 440.

Popery on the people, still continued to live in their hearts, giving unmistakable evidence the while of its undying vitality, and awaiting the destined hour of deliverance, which came at the great Reformation.

CHAPTER VI.

THE REFORMATION IN SCOTLAND.

Difference between English and Scotch Reformations—the latter simply the re-appearance of the primitive Culdee faith—hence its tenacious vitality.

The next link in the chain of this argument, brings us to a historic period, too wide to enter upon fully, but so well known that this fulness of discussion is not needed. Hence, the only proposition which we need maintain is, that *the Scottish Reformation was the simple reversal of the royal establishment of Popery in Scotland, being forced on the throne by the people, as that was forced on the people by the throne.*

This is a fact so familiar to every one, that we need adduce no proofs. Every one knows the remarkable difference between the English and Scottish Reformations in this particular. The English Reformation was forced by the Court on the people; the Scotch, by the people on the Court. There is no good reason for believing that when Henry VIII. broke with the Pope, that he might divorce his queen, a majority of the English people had any sympathy with his movement; nor indeed considering the cause of it, had they any motive for that sympathy. It is a curious fact that the religion of England has generally been the religion of the throne. It was Pagan under the Romans, Christian under the Britons, Druid under the Saxons, Papal under the Normans, Protestant under Henry, Popish under Mary, Protestant under Elizabeth, Independent under Cromwell, Prelatic under Charles II., and so continues. When no political questions were involved, the Court has never had much difficulty in securing a pretty general conformity in the matter of religion. But it has been otherwise in Scotland. It has always been strangely unmanageable in this matter. For some reason the fact is apparent, that the Scottish people have always clung with a wonderful tenacity to their religion. Hence the Reformation with them was forced by the people on the Court. Queen Mary used every agency that art, beauty, and power could wield to crush the Reformation, but although backed by the powerful aid of France, she failed, and the Reformation was forced upon the throne by the people, and became the recognised faith of the realm.

What made this striking difference between the Reformations of England and Scotland? Precisely the facts that we have been describing. This old, ancestral faith of Scotland still lived among her hills, and only awaited an opening to flame out as it did in the mighty outburst of the Reformation. The religion of the throne was the religion of their ancient hereditary enemies, of the men who had banished and butchered their gallant and godly forefathers, of whom the world was not worthy, whilst the religion of the people was the religion of the

"Scots wha had wi' Wallace bled,
Scots wham Bruce had often led,"

the old, unconquered faith of their Culdee fathers that had never bowed the knee to Baal, or acknowledged the claims of Rome. Hence although this ancient faith had been overpowered, it had never been overwhelmed. Like the sun-clad woman of the Apocalypse, she had fled from the dragon into the wilderness, and was nourished there for a time and times and a half-time: at the appointed hour the deliverance came, and a voice rang among the hills like that which sounded at the grave of Lazarus, "Loose her and let her go." And at the sound of that voice the lonely glens and heathered hills of the brave old land awaked like rough Benledi's craggy side at the whistle of Roderick Dhu, when,

"On right, on left, above, below,
Sprung up at once the lurking foe,

> And every tuft of broom gave life,
> To plaided warrior armed for strife ;"

for like some mighty gathering of the clans,

> " They came as the winds come when forests are rended,
> They came as the waves come when navies are stranded;"

and in spite of beauty, and rank, and riches, and royalty, this old ancestral faith of Iona demanded its long invaded rights, and Scotland wheeled into line a part of the sacramental host of the Church of Reformation. Was this a wonderful thing? Was it not the same old story that "truth crushed to earth shall rise again," and that

> " Freedom's battles once begun,
> Descend from bleeding sire to son,
> Though often lost are surely won."

The same fact explains the tenacity with which the Scottish people clung to their ancient and simple Culdee order against the efforts made by England to force Prelacy upon them. For a whole century that struggle continued, and was only terminated by the accession to the throne of William of Orange, a Dutch Presbyterian, who terminated the struggle and allowed the Scotch to enjoy the ancient forms of their choice. This stern resistance to Prelacy was not a spirit of political radicalism ; for when England bowed to the sword of Cromwell, Scotland took up arms for Charles II., and with his characteristic perfidy, was rewarded for her fidelity by one of the most cruel persecutions recorded in history. This terrible persecution extended to every rank, age, sex, and condition, from the kingly Argyle, who said as he walked to the scaffold, "I could die as a Roman, but I choose to die as a Christian," to servant-maids, peasants, shepherds, and even children, who were butchered by the brutal dragoons of the bloody Claverhouse, as remorselessly as the wild beast rends its prey, and with a more remorseless cruelty. The sufferings of that "killing time," when every species of torture, indignity and oppression were used, are only written fully in the book of God's remembrance. That weather-stained stone in the old Greyfriars church-yard, which records the sufferings of the Martyrs in its quaint and simple verse, states that "from May 17th, 1661, when the most noble Marquis of Argyle was beheaded, to the 17th of February, 1688, that Mr. James Renwick suffered, were one way or other murdered and destroyed for the same cause about eighteen thousand;" and yet this covers only about one-fourth of this period of struggle, and represents but feebly the agonies of unnamed and unnumbered sufferers who chose spoiling of their goods, loathsome dungeons, the boot, the thumbscrew, and death in its most terrible forms, rather than abandon the old and simple faith of their fathers, and accept the stately Prelacy that the Stuarts wished to force upon them.

Now we do not refer to their long and memorable struggle to discuss the right or wrong of either persecutors or persecuted, but to show that there must have been some very deep cause at work to generate a tenacity so unyielding as that. Why did Scotland cling to its simple, Presbyterian faith with so much indomitable firmness? How came this system to have its roots so twined around the Scottish popular heart that a hundred years of persecution could not tear them out? Not lapse of time, if this system arose with the Reformation, for the first General Assembly only met A. D. 1560, and the "tulchan bishops" were appointed in A. D. 1572, from which time the struggle against Prelacy never ceased until the accession of William and Mary in A. D. 1688. How could a new and unknown system take such root in so brief a time? You may uproot with ease the mushroom growth of a Jonah's gourd which springs up in a night and perishes in a night, but when you find some gnarled and knotted athlete of the forest that has wrestled a hundred winters with the hurricane and remained unmoved, you have found the brave old oak that has been pushing its twisting roots around the granite ribs of the

earth for a thousand years. Nothing but time
can ever generate such growths. Had the seeds
of this Presbyterian system been planted among
the hills of Scotland by the hands of Wishart,
Knox, or Melville, it had yielded at last to the
glaived hands of the sons of Anak who sought to
uproot it, for there were giants in those days. No
stripling of the forest could have retained its
hold on the soil for a hundred years of such
gigantic effort. But this was no stripling of yes-
terday. Its acorn had been planted on her misty
hills by the hands of men who gathered it from
spots where Paul planted, Apollos watered, and
John garnered the increase; and it was lodged in
a soil that was untrodden and unsubdued by the
tramp of those mailed legions of Rome that had
almost conquered the world. Its stalwart trunk
grew on apace, although "the boar out of the
wood did waste it, and the wild beast of the field
did devour it," though the fierce storm of persecution wrestled with its boughs and snapped many
of them with a martyr's bloody fate; though the
axe was laid at its root again and again, and twice
at least was it hewn to the very ground by Saxon
and Anglo-Saxon hands, yet the root still lived,
and put forth its undying vigor with a greener
growth by this terrible pruning, until it stands
to-day, the brave old Charter-oak of Christendom,

with a life so ineradicable that the gates of hell have never prevailed against it, and we trust shall never, until its topmost boughs shall catch the earliest rays of the coming of that Jesus, for whose crown and covenant so many of its offspring loved not their lives even unto the death.

The conclusion, then, to which we feel that these facts inevitably lead us is, that the religious history of Scotland can only be explained on the supposition that there was in the hearts of her people, in all the changes of her civil polity, substantially the same faith, and that this faith was that of the old Culdee and the modern Presbyterian Church, and that both therefore must be substantially the system of doctrine and order taught by the Primitive Church, and disseminated by Apostolical men.

CHAPTER VII.

CONCLUDING REFLECTIONS.

The Apostolicity of the Presbyterian Church—Simple test of Scriptural claims—Unworthy abandonment of those claims—Rule that don't work both ways—Plea for more fidelity to this old, battle-scarred Church of our fathers.

Our object in the preceding line of historical argument has been to prove, that the Presbyterian Church of the present day is a true and regular succession of the Apostolical Churches. This historical proof, however, is not essential to the validity of this claim, for it rests at last, not on History but on Scripture. All true Protestants agree with the sixth of the 39 Articles of the Episcopal Church, that " Holy Scripture containeth all things necessary to Salvation; so that whatsoever is not read therein, nor may be proved thereby is not required of any man, that it should be believed as an article of the Faith, or be thought requisite or necessary to Salvation." Now in conformity with this Article, we hold, that if the doctrines and order of the Presbyterian Church can be found in the Scriptures, that is sufficient; they are Apostolical, the doctrines and order that the Apostles ordained. If they cannot be found in the Scriptures, we give them up. Now on this point we suggest a very simple and easy test, that demands no deep scholarship. What is the Presbyterian Church? By its name, it is a Church governed by elders, in contradistinction from a Church governed by Pope, Prelates, or the Brotherhood. It is the Church of the Eldership. Now the test we suggest is to take a Concordance, and under the word Elder, examine all the texts, and see whether this is not the one, solitary feature that is common to the Church in all its dispensations. Sacraments, ritual, priesthood, prophecy, miracles, all have changed, but from the earliest trace of a Church in Genesis to the last in the Revelation, it is a Church governed by Elders, i. e. a Presbyterian Church. The oldest form of government on earth is the patriarchal, which is a government by elders, and the traces of this fact are found in all languages, where official titles embody this fact. Senior (Latin for elder,) is found in such titles as Senate, Senator, Seigneur, Sieur, Sire, Senor, Signore, Monseigneur, &c., &c., while alderman, (elderman,) Sheikh, (Elder,) and other titles of honor, all carry us back to this patriarchal fact of government by the eldest in age, which was the primitive government by elders. When this system was supplanted, and qualifications, not years were the ground of bestowal, the name remained, and the gravest and wisest, whatever their age might be, were chosen to rule, and called elders.

Now let the ordinary reader take a Concordance, and he will find upwards of one hundred texts speaking of government by elders, running through the entire Bible. Eliezer, who is called "the eldest servant of the house of Abraham," (Gen. xxiv: 2,) is in the Hebrew, called, "his servant, the *elder* of his house," i. e. the *ruler* of his house. We read of the elders of Egypt, and Pharaoh's house, called senators in Ps. cv: 22. The opening of the Exodus discovers to us elders who governed and represented the people, and through the forty years, God and Moses always dealt with the people through their representatives, the elders, and never in their primary capacity. After their settlement in Canaan, the whole people were governed by national elders, each tribe by tribe elders, each district and city, by their elders, and through the Psalms and Prophets this fact is easily recognized. The government of the Old Testament Church was by elders, i. e. Presbyterian. When the New Testament opens we find this system still existing, and every synagogue, (which was the parish church among the Jews,) governed by elders. Hence when the Apostolic Churches were founded they were framed after the synagogue model, (as the first scholars of the English Church admit,) and governed by elders, and when Peter and John speak of themselves in their old age, they call themselves elders, (1 Pet. v: 1: 2 and 3 John, v: 1,) as if this was their permanent title of office, the highest one known in the Church; and when John caught a glimpse of the Church in heaven, (Rev. iv: 4, &c.,) he saw four and twenty seats around the throne and upon them four and twenty elders, corresponding to the twelve tribes of the Old Testament Church, and the twelve Apostles of the New, as if to intimate to us this truth, that the only invariable feature of the visible Church on earth, the one unchanging fact found in every form of it is, that it is the Church of the Eldership; and wherein this differs from saying that it is a Presbyterian Church, we are not well able to see. Here then is a simple test of the scriptural character of a Presbyterian Church, which any one can apply. All that we ask is, that the test of Scripture be applied and abided by, when made. Surely this is fair. When we wish to know whether an individual is a true Christian, we do not consult his genealogical register, to know whether his ancestors were all Christians, we simply compare him with the marks of a Christian found in Scripture, and if he has them, we call him a true Christian.

So when we would know whether a Church is a true Church, as it is simply a corporation of Christians, we pursue the same course and enquire whether it has the marks of a Church found in Scripture; if it has, we call it a true Church. If we have all that the Bible requires, we are satisfied, and if we have as the very distinctive feature of our Church, the only invariable feature of the Church of God since it was organized, in government by elders, it is certainly a curious use of terms to say that Presbyterianism or government by Presbyters, is a novelty.

But as there are some who think that we undervalue this historical connection with the Primitive Church, because we do not possess it, we have given the facts on this point, known to the well-read theologian, but unknown to many others. We do not need in our relation to other Protestant churches to go further back than the Reformation, for our succession is to say the least, just as good as theirs; and when they have settled this question with the Church of Rome, we will settle it with them. But we have another reason for not feeling anxious about this question, viz: our succession runs back, independent of Rome entirely, and can be traced to the very days of the Apostles. This we have done in the preceding investigation. We have shown that Christianity was planted in Scotland near to, or during the lives of the Apostles, by Eastern and not Western Christians; that its forms and doctrines were essentially Presbyterian, and Protestant, a government by elders, and a resistance of Rome; that after a struggle of five hundred years, it was driven out of its ancient seats in the centres of population and power, and Popery forced on the people by the throne; that it still continued to exist in the rural and mountainous districts during the four hundred years of Romish occupancy; that it came forth at the Reformation and reversed the establishment of Popery, the people forcing the Reformation on the throne; and that in its strange tenacity of these ancient and simple forms and tenets, it exhibits traits that can only be explained by the admission of the fact, that this old, unconquered and unconquerable faith of their fathers never died out of the Scottish heart, and that hence the Reformation Church of Scotland, and all offshoots from that of like faith and order, are simply productions of that ancient, primeval Christianity that was planted in Scotland during Apostolical time, by Apostolical men, and that therefore we have a historical, as well as a scriptural right to claim to be regarded and treated as an Apostolical Church. In making these claims, we have no word of disparagement for any other Christian Church, or any desire to detract from their claims to honour and love. Indeed we have used their testimony in establishing these claims, and have peculiar pleasure in being able to show that we make no historical claim for our brave old mother Church of Scotland that has not been conceded by the ripest scholars of her younger and statelier sister, the Church of England.

We have presented this historical argument at this time, because we believe there is a special need for it. There is a growing tendency amongst our people, and especially our young people, to give in to the exclusive claims of other Churches to Apostolical authority, and to concede some species of inferiority to the Presbyterian Church in this matter, that is working us serious injury. Much of this is our own fault in not asserting our rightful claims as others do, and in acting on a spurious liberality that is not genuine liberality so much as indifference. It is a curious fact, that we have, with a large part of the world, the name of being exclusive and bigoted, and yet so little of the reality, that we suffer both from the name and absence of the thing which it designates. If we were really bigoted and exclusive, we would have the benefit that results from banding together and giving each other mutual support, and might patiently submit to the name, from the usefulness

of the reality. But the fact is well known to
every intelligent member of our Church, that we
have less *Church* feeling, less *esprit-du-corps*, less
of that cohesive loyalty to the Church, which has
evoked such noble activity in other Churches,
than any family of Christians in the visible
Church. Other Churches set us a praiseworthy
example in this respect. They cling together,
and grow, because they do thus hold together.
When they can attend service in a church of their
own faith, they usually do it, many of them always. But in many places our Presbyterian people, if their own church building is closed, feel
no such obligation, but almost seem to prefer to
attend some other denominational service, and
sanction their children doing so, by which tastes
are often formed, which in the end lead those
children away from their own Church. Other
Churches take special pains to invite strangers to
their services, and show them that they are welcome, but a stranger may come to some of our
churches for months, and never receive a solitary intimation of welcome, or a single assurance
that he is not regarded as an intruder. Other
Churches support their own schools, and other
Church institutions, more faithfully, we appre-
hend than is done by our people. Our children
are sent to schools, Sunday and week-day schools,

under other denominational influences, where they are not trained to love their own Church, and perhaps trained to exactly the reverse; taught insensibly, if not intentionally, to admire and love other religious forms, and then when it turns out that they desire to unite with other Churches, we are very much surprised that they have become just what they were educated to be, and that the tree has inclined just as the twig was bent. Other Churches are careful about the reading that is given to their children. Our people are so confident of the power of truth, that they do not take the trouble of even seeing that it is sown in the minds of their children, and expect a harvest, without sowing the seed. Other Churches demand of their members that their best and first energies be given to them, and only what is left to the outside claims, but many of our laymen are so absorbed with outside work, that they have hardly any time left to the peculiar work of their own Church. In these and a hundred other ways, the high claims of the Church are lowered and set aside, and she suffers from this indifference severely, and pays the penalty in an annual drain of members drawn off to other Churches, not from conviction, or change of opinion, but from mere sentiment and accidental associations.

There is another form of this practical surrender of our Church claims, that is becoming so important a matter, that it is high time for some one to speak out, and call attention to it. The Romish Church requires that in mixed marriages, the Protestant must promise to allow the children to be trained in that Church. Among Protestants the practical rule formerly was, that in such cases the wife went with the husband, as the head of the household, unless she was a communicant and he not, in which case the practice was variable. This rule of give and take was one of mutual concession, and on the whole worked fairly. But for years a silent and almost unobserved change has taken place, by which the practical rule is, that the Presbyterian must *always* give up, and the concession be made only from the one side. The result of this is that in many cases, one by one, our best young men, as well as women, are drawn off from our communion, because they are unwilling to take the firm stand about the matter of Church, which is taken by the other party. The extent of this drain on our Church would startle us were the facts brought out in detail. We know a single church, that is probably a fair sample of the whole, where we can count more than thirty of such marriages, in which the non-Presbyterian party has steadily refused to come over, and in more than half the cases, the Presbyterian has yielded, either sooner or later, and gone over to the other Church. Now here are upwards of fifteen families from one congregation lost to the Presbyterian Church, not by change of opinion, but by other causes. Probably if every church in our connection were examined, in many of them nearly the same proportion would be found to exist. Now when we remember that each of these families will in a few years represent growing circles of children, and that here is a loss for which we have no corresponding gain, the aggregate becomes very large, and it is time that we examine into this steady and silent drain of our very best blood, that is quietly going on all over our territory.

We are aware of the practical difficulties that surround this matter, and how painful it must sometimes be to take a decided stand. But we insist, that in view of existing facts, fidelity to our holiest relations demands that we take this stand, and maintain the equality of our Church with all others. Surely it is unreasonable and wrong to sanction this one sided and unequal rule of action. If it is a matter of conscience, must the Presbyterian only have no conscience? If a matter of concession, why must the Presbyterian always be the one to succumb? Are we faithful to our Church, if we allow a seeming stigma like this to be placed upon her ? Ought we not to stand up as firmly for our old, ancestral Church, as others do for theirs ? Were this a mere matter of expediency, we would say nothing about it, but, as it stands, it rises to a matter of principle. It is simply the practical question whether the Presbyterian Church stands on an equality with other Churches. If it does, we have a right to demand reciprocity, and when that reciprocity is refused, we are bound, by the most sacred of all ties, to vindicate our old mother Church from this implied allegation of inferiority. If members of other Churches think that changing Church relations is wrong, it is just as wrong in us as it is in them, unless we concede that ours is not so really a true Church as theirs. If it is a right and noble thing in them to be faithful to their own Church, is it not equally so for us to be faithful to ours ? Do we not then inflict a wrong on our Church, by thus abandoning her so easily ? Do we not sanction an unscriptural principle in so doing ? Has not the time come when Presbyterians ought to take the same stand that other Churches have done, and keep it, until the old rule of reciprocity is resumed ? Are we not doing the cause of truth and charity a real wrong, by sanctioning such concessions ? and does not self-respect, demand of us that we claim our Church rights in this matter just as others do, and give no sanction to the implied ascription of inferiority? Will not the members of other Churches respect us more for being faithful to our Church than for abandoning it so easily? We do not blame them for the staunchness with which they cling to their Churches; indeed we rather admire it, but surely their fidelity in this matter puts our laxity in any thing but a favourable light, and raises a serious question of principle, which we ought carefully to ponder. If they are right, we are wrong; if they are wrong, we can hardly be right in yielding to what is wrong. On either horn of the dilemma our practice cannot be justified.

The point which we wish to press home on the consciences of our people is, that the time has come when we must be as faithful to our own Church, as other Christians are to theirs, or be recreant to our obligations and to our history. Other Churches are waking up to an activity and earnestness that is making the work of the Lord prosper in their hands, and are lengthening their cords and strengthening their stakes. We rejoice in this awakening, and thank God that his people are nerving themselves to come up to the help of the Lord against the mighty. But shall we be laggards in this glorious onward movement? Shall this old battle-scarred Church, that has borne the brunt of a thousand well-fought fields, be found in the rear?

Shall this blue banner that has streamed in the fore
front and smoke of the conflict, in other days, be
folded and lowered now? Never! never! Every
instinct of the heart, every memory of the past,
every exigency of the present, every hope of the
future, call upon us to awake and do our duty as
our fathers did in days gone by, that our children
may have no more reason to blush for their sires
than we have to blush for ours.

What then must we do? Do, as was done on that
bloody field, when as the shot and shell ploughed
gaps in the advancing columns, the only command
that was heard above the roar of battle was the
steady order, "close up the ranks." We must
close up the ranks, keep together, move together,
not get out of supporting distance, be shoulder to
shoulder in this glorious work of winning the
world for Jesus, that "no man take our crown."

We have given these historical statements very
much for the benefit of the young, that they may
know what a noble heritage they have in this old,
unconquered Church of their fathers, that has
never bowed the knee to Rome. We do not wish
you, young friends, to be bigots, to disparage or
dislike other Churches. We would have you love
them and honour them to the last claim they possess, and we would not rob them of a single laurel
which many of them so worthily wear. But we

would have you know how much your own mother Church has a right to your love, and we would have you love her, and love her best, because she is your own. We would have you love her best, as you love your own mother best, because she is your own, and loving her thus does not detract one line of loveliness from the face of any other who is called by this sacred name. Then be true to that Church, as long as she is true to Christ. Give her the unwasted strength of your youth. Add some new leaves to that unfading chaplet which she has worn these many generations, and "the Lord shall count, when he writeth up the people, that this man was born there. As well the singers as the players on instruments shall be there; all my springs are in thee."

www.ingramcontent.com/pod-product-compliance
Lightning Source LLC
Chambersburg PA
CBHW021417090426
42742CB00009B/1172